Contents

A Place Of Sanctuary

Sitting quietly on the patio on a moonlit night, the silence is broken by a snuffling sound. Like a little steam train, the tiny creature makes his way across the lawn, his round shape silhouetted in the dim light. Soon the snuffling turns to slurping as he tucks into a dish of tinned dog food.

Like so many other animals, the hedgehog has turned to the garden for refuge as his countryside habitat has disappeared under the plough, his food supply has dwindled under the onslaught of pesticides and herbicides, and diversity has been replaced by huge expanses of arable land, designed for machinery – not for wildlife.

The disappearance of his natural habitat means the hedgehog is becoming increasingly reliant on gardens.

The red fox, a frequent visitor to urban gardens.

The Opportunists

When survival becomes the name of the game, animals are both resourceful and adaptable. Some species have been quick to recognise that the garden, particularly one that does not rely on herbicides, pesticides and artificial fertilisers, can provide a safer and more comfortable existence than the countryside.

The grey squirrel, an alien introduction from North America, has been hugely successful at finding a niche – sadly often at the expense of the native red squirrel. The urban environment holds no terrors – it is a land of parks and gardens where rich pickings are there for the taking in the lean, winter months.

The red fox has also moved into our towns and cities, finding homes in large, suburban gardens, and a ready food supply in the neighbourhood dustbins.

In some places, even the shy and retiring badger has refused to move from his ancestral home and, surrounded by concrete, he continues to eke out an existence assisted by sympathetic garden owners.

DID YOU KNOW?

While many of our wild habitats continue to decline, gardens are actually increasing and are now an important habitat in their own right.

Guess Who's Coming To Dinner?

Animals, unlike birds, are not so visible in the garden. Most, with the exception of the grey squirrel, tend to come out during the hours of darkness, and so it is important to provide food at the right time – and in the right season.

For example, there is little point in putting down food for the hedgehog in mid-winter, when he is safely tucked up in a deep sleep. However, when he wakes in spring, hungry and thin, a little help is much appreciated. In the autumn, he will need your help again, so that he can put on weight prior to hibernation. This is particularly important for youngsters born late in the year. If they do not put on enough weight, they will not survive the winter.

The objective with all garden animals should be to help them out in the hard times without allowing them to become totally dependent.

Which animals can we expect to find in the average suburban garden, and what should we feed them?

The Hedgehog

The hedgehog is the prime candidate for tinned dog and cat food, although there is a tinned hedgehog food available in some pet stores. A special dry-food mix, containing meat, insects,

DID YOU KNOW?

Bread and milk is bad for hedgehogs. They cannot digest the milk properly and it makes them ill.

Tinned dog or cat food should be on the hedgehog menu.

The grey squirrel is a master of monopolising bird feeders.

berries and cereals, has also been designed for hedgehogs, but remember to supply a bowl of water when feeding dry foods to wild animals.

The Fox

Foxes will eat most kitchen scraps, just like a pet dog.

The Badger

Badgers are partial to peanuts and raisins, and, for a treat, some are very partial to honey. Proprietary dried mixes are also available.

The Grey Squirrel

The grey squirrel hardly needs encouraging, and if you feed the birds, he will happily join in. Peanuts are a particular favourite.

The woodmouse loves hazelnuts.

The Woodmouse

The attractive woodmouse, along with the bank vole and the now rare dormouse, like peanut and hazelnuts but will only take them after dark.

Insects

Beekeepers often supplement their bees' winter feed with sugar solution, and, in the spring, this can be used as a ploy to keep over-wintering butterflies, like the peacock and small tortoiseshell, in the garden.

- Dishes of sugar solution may also be visited by bees, wasps and ants.
- Nocturnal moths are partial to black treacle painted on a suitable tree trunk.

DID YOU KNOW?

The grey squirrel is a great hoarder and buries nuts in the garden. It is probably responsible for many of Britain's self-set native trees.

Sugar solution may persuade butterflies, such as the Painted Lady to stay.

- Purpose-built ladybird and butterfly feeders, together with suitable attractant solutions, can be purchased.

Uninvited Guests

You put out your animal feed at dusk and in the morning it has gone, but how do you know you are not just feeding the local cats and the odd stray dog? Worse still, your good intentions could be fuelling a local explosion in the brown rat population – a creature that is well able to look after itself!

If you are feeding at night:

- Place the food close to the house.
- Try to find a place in the shadows of an outside light so you can watch for the creature to arrive.

Both hedgehogs and foxes will come for food placed in the light, and, after a few visits, will appear at the same time, night after night.

Putting food out for the local wildlife could mean you are unwittingly supporting the brown rat population.

Setting Up Home

Lace-wings are useful at keeping aphid numbers in check.

Now you have encouraged an animal to visit your garden, the next step is to get it to stay by providing some shelter. An animal must have somewhere where it feels safe and secure during the periods when it sleeps. The growing interest in garden wildlife has led to the manufacture of some custom-built homes.

Haven For Hedgehogs

A hedgehog house and nesting box is now available, consisting of a chamber with a lead-in tunnel to keep out dogs, foxes and badgers. The living area measures about 13 inches by 12 inches by 16 inches (33 cms by 30 cms by 40.5 cms), giving the animals plenty of room.

To start with, partially fill the nest chamber with dry leaves and grass, making sure the vent is clear. Place in a quiet corner of the garden, and cover it with compost or soil. With luck, the hedgehogs will find it and set up home.

Alternatively, you could build your own hedgehog home using marine ply, but remember it is unlikely to be used unless it is completely waterproof.

Living Space For Lacewings

Lacewings – delicate insects about 1 inch (2.5cms) long with large membranous wings – are important in

A lace-wing 'hotel' could be a life-saver in the winter. Courtesy – CJ Wildbird Foods

the fight against garden pests like aphids.

A lacewing hotel, consisting of a wooden box containing several chambers, will provide winter hibernation quarters and significantly increase their chances of survival.

A simple, home-made, waterproof box, packed with lengths of bamboo, corrugated paper or straw, will be just as good, and will become home to other insects, such as ladybirds, as well.

Bat Room

Bats eat insects on the wing, so although you cannot supply them with food, you can provide a home for roosting and hibernating.

In fact, these tiny, delicate mouse-like creatures may already be living in your attic or the eaves of the house. But, in addition, you can provide bat boxes. These are of similar construction to nest boxes for birds, but they have a slit entrance in the bottom.

You will need to install several boxes in different situations round the garden if you are to have any success, as bats are much more particular than birds.

Bats are fussy about where they live, so you may need to fit several boxes before they will move in.

Mouse House

Edible dormice, common in the counties around London, may be enticed into a side-entry bird-box style home, fixed to a suitable tree trunk.

The tiny harvest mouse is less likely to move into your garden, but it has been known for them to take up residence in a tennis ball with a hole in the side.

Bee-line

Bumblebees often build their nests in old mouse holes but you can help them by providing a wooden underground chamber, lined with moss. The nest must be covered with 10 mm wire mesh to protect it from marauding mice which love to eat the developing bees.

Bees are welcome additions to any garden.

A badger is no respecter of boundaries and won't mind whose lawn he uses to forage for worms.

Providing shelter and supplementary food is no guarantee that you will keep animals in the garden.

Animals need a habitat that provides for all their needs all the time – a place where they can live, breed and rear their young, generation after generation. With a few exceptions, the average back garden cannot do this.

However, before rushing out to convert your garden into a multi-purpose wildlife habitat, you must remember that wildlife is no respecter of boundaries and fences. The badger you have painstakingly attracted to your garden is a free spirit, and there is every chance that he will try the neighbour three doors down to see if there are any easy pickings.

The success you have in attracting animals to your garden (unless it is very large) is more dependent on the suitability of the area as a whole, than it is on your efforts within your own tiny patch. A small wildlife haven, without safe corridors allowing the wildlife to come and go, is no better than a prison.

Fortunately in most areas, groups of gardens make ideal wildlife habitats, and there are many things that can be done to make these habitats more wildlife friendly.

If you look at the average garden, it is, in fact, full of dangers for potential animal residents. Before embarking on major improvement projects, it makes sense to eliminate some of these hazards.

Nylon Netting

One of the biggest killers in the garden is nylon netting, used to protect fruit from birds, or to keep herons and cats out of ponds. It can entangle snakes, amphibians and hedgehogs; and because it does not 'give', the more they struggle, the more entangled they become.

Be especially vigilant when mowing the lawn, as some animals have excellent camouflage and may be difficult to spot.

Mowing and Strimming

Careless mowing and strimming are also high on the list of hazards. This is particularly the case if the grass is long, or has not been cut recently, giving animals a chance to move in.

Hedgehogs and frogs are the most common victims. Toads are also very vulnerable because, instead of moving away, they tend to remain stationary and try to flatten themselves against the ground.

Grass snakes often lay their eggs in compost heaps.

Bonfires

If you build a pile for a bonfire over a period of time, it will become a temporary home for frogs, toads, hedgehogs and many other insects. Put a match to it – and many creatures are likely to be roasted alive.

Compost Heap

Compost heaps are favoured by many animals because of the extra warmth generated. Grass snakes, in particular, often lay their eggs in compost heaps. Woodmice build their nests in the dry outer layers, and the occasional hedgehog will curl up in the corner for a daytime nap. Slow worms love to bask in the sunshine on top of a compost heap.

Take extra care when forking through your compost heap to avoid disturbing wildlife – or worse still, spearing a creature with your fork.

Garden Hazards

Predators

Predators can be a major problem in the garden, with the domestic cat being wildlife enemy No. 1. Well known for catching birds, cats are also efficient killers of mice, shrews, voles, moles, and particularly frogs at spawning time.

Dogs don't catch as much wildlife, but they can cause a lot of disturbance, particularly for the shy, larger animals like foxes and deer.

The cat is public enemy number one to many wildlife animals, wreaking havoc wherever he hunts.

Rubbish

General household rubbish, like the plastic collars from four-packs of canned drinks, can easily entangle an inquisitive hedgehog, and many a hedgehog has got its head stuck in a tin can or a yoghurt pot.

Carelessly discarded bottles and jam-jars can trap mice and voles because the sides are too slippery for them to climb.

DID YOU KNOW?

The slow worm is neither slow, nor is it a worm. It is, in fact, a lizard without legs.

Garden Pond

Although all animals can swim, many drown in ponds and pools because the sides are too steep for them to climb out. A special ramp can be fitted, or if you are planning a new pond, design it with a walk-out pebble area.

Many animals drown when they fall into a pond which they can't get out of. Fit a ramp to give them an escape route.

Poisons

Even in the wildlife-friendly garden there are toxic chemicals. Creosote and slug pellets are obviously harmful, but so are simple things like salt, which can kill a toad in a matter of hours if it gets on to his skin.

Common toad: salt is hazardous to toads.

Go Organic

The first step in turning your garden into an animal-friendly habitat, where wildlife will choose to stay, is to go organic.

By adopting organic principles and growing methods, you start to build food chains – and the longer you can make these chains, the larger the animals you will attract.

Most of the animals you want to attract are near the top of the food chain and rely on the members lower down for sustenance. In the natural world, the rules of supply and demand apply. The numbers of animals will rise as the food supply increases, then fall as it decreases. Unfortunately, it does not change overnight and you will have to be patient.

Avoiding pesticides will help you to keep many of your garden visitors.

Start by throwing away pesticides, as these not only kill the pests but also many of the beneficial insects and tiny creatures in the garden – all of which are valuable food for the animals we want to attract. If the hedgehog eats slugs and snails poisoned by chemical slug baits, these will build up in its body with potentially harmful effects.

Stop using inorganic fertilisers. In fact, the benefit to your garden is reduced as some of the fertiliser is lost as it leaches down into the subsoil, eventually polluting watercourses or your garden pond.

Best Of Both Worlds

Build a compost heap – everybody wins with a compost heap.

- It provides a home for many garden animals.
- It converts garden rubbish into a usable resource, which improves soil structure and increases the numbers of tiny animals present.
- It is a source of food for growing plants.
- When spread over the soil, it helps to retain moisture.
- After dark, mice, voles and shrews, together with frogs, toads and newts, find sustenance amongst the compost.

A compost heap is an essential part of an eco-friendly garden.

Go Organic

Planting Out

Grow as many different plants as you can – from annual bedding plants to trees, which will live for 50 years or more.

A **vegetable patch**, containing a mix of cabbages, root crops (e.g. carrots, and parsnips), beans, as well as salad plants (e.g. lettuce and radish), will support a greater range of creatures than the same area covered with potatoes.

A small **shrubbery**, containing nectar-producing shrubs like buddlea and hebe, mulched with bark chippings, will be more productive than the equivalent area laid to gravel or concrete.

The greater the variety of plants, the more diverse the wildlife you will attract. Pictured: mixed vegetable and flower gardening.

Control Measures

If you garden organically, occasionally a pest species will multiply more quickly than your beneficial predators can deal with it.

In this case, you will need to give nature a helping hand by using one of the many specific biological controls available.

- A nematode (tiny worms) can be sprayed on the ground to kill slugs and snails without harming the hedgehog.
- Tiny wasps can be introduced to control whitefly or red spider mite.
- There is a bacterium which will kill the cabbage white caterpillar without harming other caterpillars.

Pond Life

Different animals require different habitats according to their needs. Although you are unlikely to be able to simulate a sandy heath to attract sand lizards and smooth snakes to your garden, there is, nevertheless, a great deal that can be done within the confines of a small plot.

Nearly every animal requires water to drink; some like to bathe, while for others it is an essential part of their life cycle.

Providing a regular supply of water will result in more animals visiting your garden. Providing a pond with an adjacent boggy area will persuade some to stay.

DID YOU KNOW?

There are more than 2 million garden ponds in the UK – but there is still room for more.

A pond will provide hours of pleasure.

Pond Life

Choosing a Site

If you are going to the trouble and expense of building a pond, and you want to make sure it is as wildlife-friendly as possible, you will need to think more in terms of the animals' needs rather than your own needs.

A good view from the patio, while desirable, may not fulfil the needs of some of the more shy creatures. The ideal site is a south-west-facing corner, with some shrubbery for cover for approaching animals, and low cover for emerging amphibians.

It should be a level site which receives sunshine for at least five hours each day, with an approach from an adjacent lawn or path on one side.

Common frog: it won't be long before your new pond has visitors.

Size Matters!

The bigger the pond, the larger the number of species it will attract – but even a small pond is better than no pond at all.

Once you have decided upon the position and approximate size of your pond, mark out the shape using sand. Remember, the simpler the shape – round or oval – the easier it will be to fit the liner.

Even more important than the shape is the profile. Part of the pond needs to be at least 3 ft (91 cms) deep so that wildlife can survive beneath a thick coat of ice. But it also needs areas of shallow water which will warm up quickly in the spring, sloping back gradually to dry land with easy access for drinking and bathing.

Get Digging

Before you start digging, put in level pegs round the perimeter because, if the pond is not level, lots of liner will show on the high side and the final volume of the pond will be considerably reduced.

Nothing goes to waste in a wildlife-friendly garden, and the spoil can be used to create a rockery or bank elsewhere.

When the digging is completed:

- Smooth the sides and remove any sharp objects.
- Line the pond with underlay, old carpet, or even cardboard to protect the liner.
- Fit the liner and smooth into shape.
- Cover with three to four inches of soil.
- Build a pebble area in the shallows and slowly fill with water.

The Plants

Leave for a few days before planting with a selection of native plants.

- In deep water, anchor clumps of oxygenators like hornwort and water violet.
- Floaters, like fringed water lily and amphibious bisort, also require deep water, but their leaves will cover the surface, helping to reduce the light and control algal growth.

Common frog on a lily pad: pond vegetation is vital to support all aspects of pond life.

Pond Life

You may be lucky enough to attract a great crested newt to your pond.

- Round the edge in the shallows, bog bean and flowering rush will do well.
- The boggy area will support yellow iris, water mint and lesser spearwort.

The Animals Move In

As the plants establish themselves, the animals will start to move in. There is a good chance that common frogs will breed in the first or second year, and toads, even if they don't breed, will find plenty of food in the boggy area.

Common and palmate newts may breed, and, if you are really lucky, the larger great crested newt could become a regular springtime visitor.

This large concentration of amphibians may well attract predators like the grass snake, and mammals such as the fox and the muntjac deer may call in for a drink.

Ponds are also vital for many of our insects, like the beautiful dragon and damselflies, as well as mayflies, alderflies and caddisflies, which, in turn can attract insect-eating bats.

A pond may also encourage the muntjac deer to visit.

Wild Flower Meadows

When your tadpoles turn into tiny frogs, they will spend the next three or four years away from the pond. They will need food and shelter, and one of the best habitats for them is a wild flower meadow. This attracts lots of tiny insects, offers shade from the sun, and provides places to hide from predators.

Choosing a Site

The closer the meadow is to the pond, the better. But the most important factor is for the soil not to be too fertile. To achieve this, it may be necessary to strip the topsoil before making a seedbed using the subsoil.

The meadow can then be sown with a mixture of grasses and perennial wildflowers such as knapweed, bird's foot trefoil, cranesbill and ox eye daisy, together with some annuals like poppies which will give a great show in the first year.

Wild flower meadows offer ideal protection for a number of wild species.

Meadow Life

Apart from the amphibians – frogs, toads and newts – the meadow will probably attract voles. These are tiny creatures, such as the short-tailed field vole, which will build its nest just below the surface and tunnel in the dense mat of grasses at soil level. An unlikely visitor could be the small but attractive harvest mouse.

Natural Hedges

The short-tailed field vole enjoys a meadow habitat.

A hedgerow can be a hive of activity. Pictured: grey squirrel feeding at the bottom of a hedge.

There are few gardens large enough to support an area of woodland, but it is possible to create a useful habitat by planting a hedge using a mixture of native species of trees and shrubs. If the hedge can be incorporated into a grassy bank, so much the better.

Plant a mixture of crab-apple, beech, dog rose, elm, hawthorn, hazel, bramble and holly. These will supply nectar for butterflies, food and nesting sites for many species of birds, plus food and shelter for some animals.

- Hedgehogs may hibernate in the hedge bottom when it thickens up.
- The bank vole may move in, making tunnels in the bank, and feeding on the plentiful supply of hips, haws, berries and fruit.
- The woodmouse may be attracted to the hazelnuts and berries.

Understanding Bats

On warm, summer evenings as dusk falls it is not unusual to see bats flying noiselessly through the air, using their built-in sonar to guide them round objects as they hunt tirelessly for flying insects. The chances are that you will be watching the Pipistrelle, the smallest of our 14 species of bats. In the south of England, you may see the Lesser Horseshoe bat; if you live near water, you may see the Daubentons bat skimming over the surface.

The pipistrelle is the smallest of UK bats.

Understanding Bats

Like many of our native animals, these tiny, furry, mouse-like creatures need all the help they can get, as some of the British bats are now extremely rare. Sadly, the bat is much misunderstood. To set the record straight:

- Bats are small, clean creatures which do not smell.
- They do not build nests, or gnaw wiring if they set up home in your attic.
- Their droppings are dry and disease-free.
- No bat would deliberately become entangled in your hair.
- British bats do not suck blood as they are entirely insectivorous.

A bat box should have saw cuts at the bottom to assist the bat's grip when entering his nest.

A Place To Roost

The best way to help bats is to install bat boxes which they may use for roosting, hibernation or breeding. This is especially important as their natural roosts in hollow trees disappear.

A bat box is constructed from rough sawn wood about 1 inch (2.5 cm) thick. It is about the same size as a bird box, and has a slit about ¾ inch (2 cm) wide along the bottom to allow entry.

The box should be fixed high on a tree, or in the gable end of a house, where it can receive sunshine for a few hours each day.

Flying Food

Bats feed solely upon insects, including flies, midges, beetles, moths, caddis flies and mayflies.

Apart from maintaining a pond which will give a regular supply of hatching insects, the number and variety of insects in the garden can be increased by growing night-scented flowers, and by leaving a light on after dark to bring in the moths.

Natural Habitats

I f you are short of space, a log pile is a habitat which does not need to take up too much room. All you need are a couple of barrow-loads of old logs. It is best if they are partially rotten, and of different sizes and species. Simply form them into a jumbled pile, sited reasonably close to the pond if you have one, and leave them alone.

A log pile is a simple but effective measure to attract wildlife.

Colonisation Begins

As the logs rot, they will be colonised by all sorts of creatures, and will become a mini-habitat in their own right.

- Millipedes, centipedes and wood lice will hide under the bark.
- Beetle grubs will bore into the wood as the mosses and fungi start to take hold.
- Some of this year's crop of young frogs will move in, making it their home for at least the next 12 months.
- The local toad will find somewhere in the middle to hibernate.
- Woodmice, shrews and voles will find natural food among the logs which will also give them protection from predators.

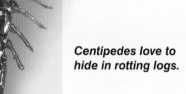

Centipedes love to hide in rotting logs.

Gradually the pile will become smaller as it rots, so add a few more logs each year to keep it going.

The Lucky Few

If your garden is situated in the right natural habitat, it may well be visited by animals not normally associated with gardens or garden feeding.

- The cottage which borders a river or stream may have regular sightings of the otter.

If you live by a river, you may be lucky enough to have a bank vole (above) or otter (top) passing through.

- Water voles may live in the river banks close to the house.
- The now common mink will pass through in the night, helping itself to your chickens if they are not secured.
- If you live in the Scottish highlands, some bread and jam on your bird table could make the rare pine marten a frequent visitor after dark.
- Edible dormice are fairly common in the home counties, often spending the winter in bird boxes.
- If you live in the north or west beyond the range of the grey squirrel, then the beautiful red squirrel may be attracted to your table.

All an animal needs is the right conditions and it will move in, often regardless of the close proximity of human habitation. The thing is, you never know what may turn up!

The Nimbys *('Not in my backyard')*

Among our animals, there is a few which, depending upon circumstances, you would prefer to discourage.

- The brown rat, a carrier of diseases like leptospirosis, should be actively discouraged.
- If you live in the country, rabbits, particularly the youngsters, look great in the field next door, but they can do a great deal of damage in the garden, digging holes in flower beds and eating plants.
- Draw back the curtains and view a lawn covered with piles of earth and your love for the mole will quickly evaporate.
- If your garden has been built over a badger path, it would make sense to provide a proper entrance and exit or they will make their own.

> **DID YOU KNOW?**
>
> *The common goldfish loves to eat tadpoles and other small pond creatures.*

Rabbits can wreak havoc in your garden.

The Controversial Squirrel

Of all our animals, the grey squirrel is probably the most problematic.

Once grey squirrels find a source of food, they are persistent and resourceful. Most people enjoy watching their antics, but they can consume or store large amounts of food often intended for other mouths or beaks.

Although they look cute sitting on a stump and eating peanuts, squirrels also have a very destructive side. If they decide that your loft is the place to live, then watch out for damaged pipes and electric wiring.

Your dustbin could even come under attack if the squirrels are very hungry.

The best course of action is to discourage them from coming too close to the house. If they are eating too much bird food, try a squirrel-proof feeder or dust the food with chilli pepper. It will not harm the birds but the squirrels do not like it.

The Aliens

There is another group of animals which we must not encourage and these are the aliens. The ninja turtle craze of the early nineties left many red-eared terrapins and snapper turtles in our ponds, particularly in larger ponds in built-up areas.

Bullfrog tadpoles are sometimes offered for sale through aquatic outlets. Resist the temptation to rehouse one of these in your garden pond. Not only is it illegal, but they will eat all the resident wildlife.

The red-eared terrapin (top left) and the snapping turtle (above) were introduced to ponds following the ninja turtle craze.

Who Has Been Visiting The Garden?

We all know when the grey squirrel has been visiting, bold as brass, he sits there eating peanuts and monopolising the feeders.

However, most of the other animal visitors are shy or nocturnal, and if you see one during the day then it may be sick or injured.

Keeping Watch

If you are patient, you should be able to watch hedgehogs coming to feed. Many of the larger animals, like foxes and badgers, will follow a set pattern, so, if you can find out 'when and where', you can watch them from a distance almost any day.

You may get a glimpse of the woodmouse as it steals peanuts from the bird table, its large eyes shining in the torchlight, before it jumps for cover.

Walking quietly round the garden after dark with a torch allows you

You'll be amazed at the variety of wildlife that emerges after dark.

to catch up with the amphibians and reptiles. This is particularly good on warm, damp nights when frogs, newts and toads are out feeding. It is also possible to get very close to frogs and toads during the breeding season when they wait for hours on end with their heads above water.

Who Has Been Visiting The Garden?

Snakes and slow worms love to bask in the sun on sheltered banks or on a compost heap. Remember they are slow in early spring but by mid-summer they will be gone before you are close enough to see them.

Look for clues – the tops of these hazelnut shells have been removed by woodmice.

Tell-tale Signs

There are other signs you can look for which will tell you if an animal has been in the garden.

- Bark removed from trees indicates rabbits or squirrels.
- Shells from hazelnuts could mean dormice, woodmice, bank voles or squirrels.
- Small nests made from dry grass, hidden in sheds or woodpiles, tell you it's a woodmouse or house mouse.
- If the nest is in the grass, it may be a short-tailed field vole or even a harvest mouse.
- Tunnels in a bank or compost heap, with worn runs, mean you may have a rat problem.

A nest in the grass could signal the presence of a harvest mouse.

Play Detective

Check the lawn for animal droppings, those of hedgehog or fox are quite distinctive and those of deer, rabbits, rats and mice can be identified with practice.

Have a look at the edge of the pond for foot prints – is it a fox or a dog?

Always check out the garden after a snowfall as you may get a few surprises and find out where some of our creatures of the night are spending their days.